A Journey of the Heart and Soul

Poetry to Inspire and Sustain

S. E. BLACKSTOCK

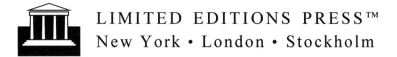

LIMITED EDITIONS PRESS™
New York • London • Stockholm

Acknowledgements

In a day and age when I thought chivalry was long dead, I met a man with intelligence, kindness, warmth, and manners. And if that was not enough, he tipped his hat to me.

Well, right then and there I decided that I needed to know this man better. And since we were in cyberspace, I became his Scarlett O'Hara, and delightfully to my surprise, the dear man had a sense of humor, and became my Rhett Butler.

And even more to my surprise, Bill writes poetry, and he has graciously allowed me to include his lovely poem "A Single, Perfect, Rose" here:

When I look into your eyes, feelings will come, I know.

Thoughts and words that I must hide, and never ever show.

But rest assured, there is one thing, you'll always be to me.

As beautiful and precious, as any flower can be.

Thank you, Bill McGee, for being a truly dear friend.

I have met many people in my life, but few have made me feel quite as special as a small handful that I have met on the polling website *SodaHead*.

Such is Don Odom, the wonderful publisher of this book. He has opened doors in my mind that have been closed for many years. He has opened vistas that once were obscured, providing a 360-degree view.

Don, thank you for all the different doors to wonderland you have opened for this Alice, and you know where they all lead.

S. E. Blackstock

"Jes"

a gentle hand

He rode into my life on a white horse,
That was how I knew he was one of life's good guys
With flowers and gentle hands, did he capture my attention
With his words and his convictions did I see that he was wise

In agreeing to disagree, did he secure my interest
And again, with his opinions, did he rekindle my compassion
For the downtrodden, a trait that was almost buried with time

With each conversation, he became more dear
And with his humor, he made me laugh
Laughter being healing for the soul

And with his heart for equality for all, the working man,
The elderly, the people of color, and the steadfastness with which he
Stood for them, did he earn my respect.

But it is His love of God that placed him in my heart.
And makes me proud
to call him friend

Karma go round

Round and round she goes
lifetime to lifetime
the circle grows

How many times will it
take to learn?

You hurt me
I hurt you back

The Karma go round
rickety rack

Well my dear, I'm jumping off
I'd rather love you
than hurt you again

So come back my love
lets try it again
with kindness and gentleness
forgiving the pain

The Karma go round
rickety rack
with love the two of us
could stop it in its tracks

My Uncle Ralph

A snowy mantle now sits
where raven curls once graced
a road map of joyous life gone by on his face
where future dreams once raced

Tall he stands, straight and proud
with only his words he stands out in a crowd
Because with them he honors his heavenly Father

Some wear a uniform for God and country
But it was his lady he fought for
her name is Liberty

A phantom hand rests in his today
his heart's true love
who now resides
in heaven above

He has walked through life
with head held high
no fears, no regrets,
just a life fulfilled
and a longing to hold
her hand once more

Starburst

She streaks across the night sky, one destination in mind
The arms of acceptance, where she can be herself
Where in shining, she is enhanced by another
And when embraced her aura glows

She circles the milky way
in search of the arms she knows
traveling through the universe
like a shooting star, her aura grows
And in meeting his gaze, the ecstasy bursts

The twin stars collide, bursting apart
and within, the two souls who have searched
finally together, merging into one
they dance, and they swirl,
the elation unmatched, the joy spills over
and fills the night sky with light everlasting

Claire de Lune

A gentle ride on a satin ribbon,
Over the moon, and through the stars
Skipping on sunbeams
Caressed by moonbeams
Sliding through a black hole
To land in your arms.
Circling Saturn, jumping over Mars
Just to find you and dance once more
The spirits climb higher
The souls meet and mingle
The minds have a dance of their own
The hearts are in sync
The hearts are ablaze
The hearts are intertwined as one
Tightly clutching each other
They savor the dance
Their lips meet and mingle
They enter and exit each other
And the warm breeze that blows through me
Separates me from the ills of the world

Caresses my soul
And makes my spirit soar
Once again the satin ribbon
Dips down under the milky way
And up over heaven's gates
Stopping to dance round a nebula
Skipping asteroids in my wake
Dancing with moonbeams
Then gently merging into one
Whole soul again,
leaving the spirits to begin anew

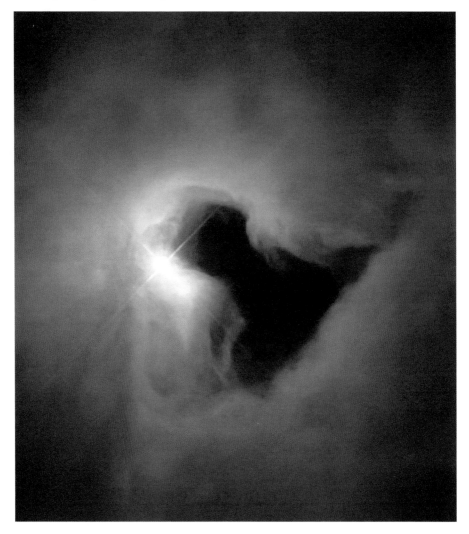

Walk with God

I've walked across the desert sands
At all times knowing I am in God's hands

I've walked thru time and
I've walked thru space
Ever mindful of God's grace

I've slept under the sky
had drinks with the guys
I've danced the night away

I've weathered the storm, for
its in storms we are born
He always brings us out the other side

In Him I will stay
In Him I'll abide
Under His wing I will hide

I've danced under the stars
caught moonbeams in a jar
but the biggest thrill of them all

Is knowing the love of the
creator above
It keeps the wind in my sails

Fluidity

She moves fluidly through time and space as if she travels on a ribbon
of silk
stopping only to smell the flowers along her journey

With clouds for stepping-stones, she glides through the stars
weaving in and out of asteroids, and skimming over limped
pools of moonlight

immersing herself in golden sunshine
then covering herself with the dark of night
as soon as she notices that you have glimpsed
her glorious body

She was there in the beginning
and she has seen the end
yet the journey remains the adventure

Will you join me?

Europa Dreams

I glide along, on the music of the universe,
feeling the embrace of every note
It surrounds me like a velvet glove
and sensuously caresses every inch of my body
and like a spring shower gently washes away all the cares of the world

As it takes me higher into the night sky
I can see the stars, in all of their radiant glory
Now jealous of the euphoria that europa wrapped me in

Gliding still further, across the milky way
another traveler I meet, to share the dance
The dance, unrehearsed, so divine, we become one
one with each other, and one with the universe
and then culminating in the explosion that is ecstasy
and melting as one, to rest, to linger
one with the music, and lost in the dream of Europa

Who am I?*

I am a lighthouse
I can see into your soul
I can shed light where shadow
has lived for years

I am thoughts on the wind
I can plant seeds in your mind
I am a mighty ocean wave
that can wash away your fears

I am a gentle summer breeze
that can dry your tears
I am a spring shower
that will make your garden of dreams grow

I am the morning dew that feeds your heart's desire
I am the twilight that turns into shades of night
to give your weary eyes rest

I am the wings that carry off your soul in the dead of night
to the safe haven of dreams and memory
and back by morning light
after riding among the stars

I am a the conviction that fills your soul
and steels you against the world

I am a broom that sweeps the cobwebs
from the corners of your mind
And I am the means with which
to drive your demons out

I am the ray of golden sunshine
that lights up your world
I am the rushing wind
that carries you to the throne of God

I am the spirit of the living God
and am here to save your soul

It's about the Holy Spirit

Facets of Discovery

There is an old wise woman in me, who wants to share the wisdom she has gathered over the years

There is a lady, prim and proper in me, who would like to take tea with the queen

There is a mother in me who wants to reach out and heal the wounds of mankind

*There is a child in me, who wants
to play, and explore wonderland,
and who still misses her Daddy*

*There is a young woman in me
who wants romantic dinners and
moonlit walks on the beach*

*There is a vixen in me that wants to grab you
and make you scream with delight*

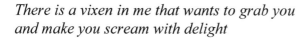

On life's journey, there are many paths, each one worth exploring

Inside Heaven's Gate

A highway of light
do we tread
petals of roses
crown our heads

closer to heaven
with each step
hand in hand
and yet in His
we stop to rest

He draws us nigh
we see our goal
it is on high
to the heart of God

on wings we ride
we take the plunge
we are overwhelmed
with joy and love
and in His light we hide

Grandfather's Eyes

First time I saw Jesus
In whom true love lies
was the first time that I gazed into
my Grandfather's eyes

He led me to the throne of God
when I was only three
I asked God to let His son
come live inside of me

Grandfather's eyes
Grandfather's eyes
I could always see Jesus
in my Grandfather's eyes

In Jesus precious name
Is how he ended every prayer

then He taught me about Jesus
and showed me how to care

Just trust in the Lord dear
everything will be just fine
is what he would always tell me
this Grandfather of mine

Grandfather's eyes
Grandfather's eyes
I could always see Jesus
In my Grandfather's eyes

Gentle Rain

It takes a gentle rain from heaven
to touch my weary soul
a pouring down of sunshine
to make my heart grow whole

the raising of a gentle breeze
to cleanse the musty air
a gentle touch from Jesus
to remind us God still cares

A gentle rain from heaven
to wash the earth anew
a rainbow on the desert
to remind us dreams come true
it takes a flower blooming
to remind us God still cares
a gentle breeze from heaven
blowing thru the air

Send the rain, send the soul cleansing rain
Dear God send your heavenly rain
brush away my tears, calm all my fears
and send your rain

Now heaven's know for miracles
seen them over and over again
the wonderful thing about miracles
never knowing where or when

It takes a gentle rain from heaven
to make a spirit grow
a sending up of praise
to set your heart aglow
it takes a stand of faith
to reap the good you've sewn
it takes the greatest love
the world has ever known

Fire

Oh Lord within this heart of mine
There burns the fires of love

A fire so bright and burning hot
that all the seas could not quench

This fire burns eternally
But not in vain I hope

For I still have you my Lord

Ecstasy

Through clouds of hazy blue, I see
Golden hues of ecstasy
A staircase to heaven
for you and me

Along a road of golden sunshine

When I look at the wonder God has created
I feel that's where we belong

I feel His kingdom should be our home
to dwell in love and beauty

Life on a Pedestal

The barroom got real quiet when she walked in through the door
I'd never seen one woman wear such luxury before
She was dressed in silk and satin diamond rings and silver mink
Now you know what a guy like me would think

So I took the stool beside her said "Hello" and ordered wine;
She asked if I was married; I said not right at the time;
So she tipped the band a twenty Had them play her favorite song;
When the chorus came around she sang along.

She sang:

Life up on a Pedestal is lonely and it's cold
I'm like a marble statuette or figurine of gold
Just a piece in his collection; Hope you think that it's alright
When I step down off the Pedestal tonight

When we left the barroom she followed my old Chevrolet
There in that motel parking lot her Rolls looked out of place
But beneath that silk and satin she was burning with desire
I did everything I could to tame the fire

When I woke up in the morning that Rolls outside was gone
I thought I had been dreamin' that the wine had put me on
But the motel office told me the bill had done been paid
And I found this note in my old Chevrolet

It said:

Life up on a Pedestal is lonely and it's cold
I'm like a marble statuette or figurine of gold
Just a piece in his collection; Hope you think it was alright
When I stepped down off the Pedestal last night

She was lonely He'd left her cold and lonely
She was only lonely Up on the Pedestal she's lonely
Somewhere tonight she's lonely

Written in collaboration with Glenn Warren, 1984

Prodigal

Here I stand
Life's prodigal child
Endlessly searching
Forever on trial

Down life's highways
and byways
Along every mile
A new trial and error
But I've learned how to smile
Tho' false it may be
No one shall know
Till love sets me free
And two hearts shall grow

1969

Souls

You talked and joked with everyone
but while you didn't notice me watching
I got a peek inside your heart
and noticed it was aching
I shed a tear and then
I looked and your soul opened up
a soul as deep as the ocean
and a spirit as tall as the sky
A caring chap, looking to heal the world
Then as soon as you saw me peeking
you climbed back inside to hide
A depth of soul, that when glimpsed
you cover and shy away
In helping other people, you don't leave enough for yourself
and when others try to help you
you don't think you are deserving

I reach out to comfort you, you turn me away
Yet you don't realize that in letting me help you, you are helping me

You are soft as a whisper, as tender as the newly fallen petals from a
rose
Yet strong as steel, forged in the fires of Vulcan
A protective knight, in shining armor
yet gentle as a summer breeze
whose caress I'd like to know

You intoxicate in rolling waves
you entice with your charm and your youth
Until I am caught in your velvet vice
Do your lips taste of honey or fine wine?

Rushing wind

I sat and watched
as a rushing wind
blew across the land today

It blew away injustices
that crippled it's own with fear
It blew away the hatred
that was formed from misunderstanding

It blew away the hate that killed
without rhyme or reason
It blew away the shadows
where death and deceit would lie in wait

It swept away the tears of a world
weary from crying
and swept away the fears of a world
tired of trembling

But last of all, and surely best
this rushing wind I watched today
blew across the hearts of men
nurturing the seeds of love
sown so long ago

Then I watched a garden bloom
the love of God once more shined
where the rushing wind had swept away the gloom

The Rushing Wind that is the Holy Spirit of the living God

God's Hand

The world is such a lovely place
Gazing on God's creations
The sky above
The grass below
My eyes in awe and jubilation
That He took His time
To make all these things
Truly the best things in life are free

1969

CAROUSEL

Love is like a carousel
It has it's ups and downs
My carousel was dragging bottom
Till you came around
Now I have happiness
That I never knew
I tingle all over
Just thinking of you
Please stay by my side
Forever and a day
Or my life
Shall surely fade away
Life is such a happy thing
Walking by your side
If you should ever leave me
Surely I would die
I love the way your eyes meet mine
And then your tender kiss
Surely no one else on earth
Could know this wondrous bliss
I love the way your hands caress my hair
Then gently let it fall
Surely in this whole world
You are the lovingness of all
I love the way you hold me tight
Whenever I am sad
For when you hold me close to you
I feel alive and glad
I love the way you lit my fire
And the way you keep it burning
Cause with you ever near me
My heart is never yearning

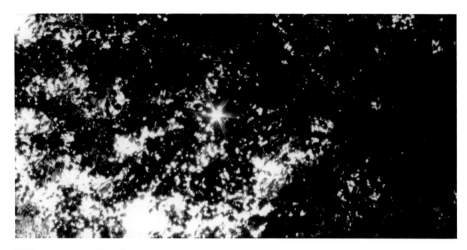

Heaven help me

As I plod along the trodden path of life
I wonder if there is anything but strife
Each time my chance for happiness comes along'
It seems mine eyes are blinded by the light
Each time the test of brain and brawn has found me
It seems my heart is swimming in a sea of false love
Heaven help me
Which way to turn
When will mine eyes
Cease to burn
Mine heart to be free
From this clutter of pain
Mine soul to be washed
From foolishness' stain
Mine ears to be closed
To lie after lie
But to be open to truth from just one guy

1969

Autumn

When Autumn leaves of
red, gold, and green

go floating slowly,
silently down the stream

and Winter steals upon the
scene
she wraps her icy tendrils
round your shoulders

Summer is a memory, and
spring but a dream

remember the warm glow
of Autumn

while the Winter snows
still gleam

Pure love

With heart in hand
I give to you
An everlasting love
In hopes that someday
Sweet and pure
Your love you'll give to me
To be shared by two
And treasured dear
Through time eternally

1969

if

is the biggest word I know
And wishing won't make my dreams come true
Hoping won't make it so
But if there is a God in heaven
And I know there is
I know that you'll want me back again
for my happiness is His

He's worked many miracles for me in the past
And it will take a miracle to give me happiness
And make it last
All I need for complete inner peace and contentment
Is the miracle of your love

All I want is one more chance
To start anew, and forget
the hurt I knew in the past

It seems that all the love in the world
Was placed within my heart
None saved for any other
So that I may receive it in return

I know that if you could love me
You would never know sorrow
For I would keep you happy through every
Sleeping and waking moment

1969

I live
for my savior

I live for my savior
because He died for me
high on a cross
for all the world to see

His humiliation and shame
provided me with salvation
and gain
in a world without mercy or
love

So I'll live for my savior
and die for my savior
and walk the path that I
chose

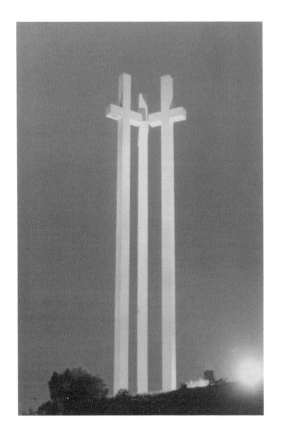

It was for my salvation
that He chose the cross
and for His sacrifice
that I chose Him

I love my savior
because He first loved me
the cross is the beginning
the crown is the end
so I will walk upright
to only Him will I bend

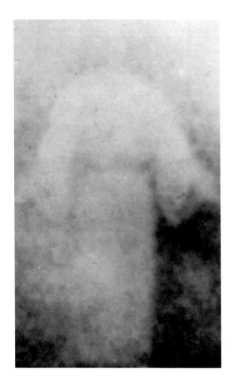

The son of God

He must have been the son of God
What other man would take such
chances
None of any sanity
and He had sanity to spare

No magician He
for all the miracles performed
were all for profit of receiver's
only

Can you imagine what
the doctor's fee might be
for healing lameness with a smile
and blindness with a wink?

And those mercenary merchants
would have jailed a man
far sooner than they did
the living walking Christ
for turning water into wine
or making one thin slice of bread
manna for the many

We're told He never cried
within the confines of ill kept stable
on that dark and silent night

Even singing was left to the angels
who but the son of God
would miss the chance to
sing in the midst of angels

A warrior's heart

A warrior's heart
will take you there
anywhere that he can care

A warrior's heart by day will fight
and no sleep will he find by night

He fights for wisdom
he fights for what's right
but the reason he fights
for all that's above
is that a warrior's heart is overflowing with love
His love of family, his love of God
his love of truth, it marches on
which makes it doubly hard to pierce
for it is his love that makes him fierce

A warrior's heart from dusk till dawn
will fight each battle till the war is won
and when at last his war is done
the warrior's heart takes root in his son

Blessings from my heart

Somewhere in Time

Somewhere in time
Don't I know you from
Somewhere in time
It seems to me that
You're too easy to love
Our fate is written in the stars above
Down through the ages
We've filled all the pages
With laughter, joy, and love
Time after time
Just new beginnings
Without any end
Somewhere in time
Don't I know you from
Somewhere in time
I know those eyes
And I know that smile
Together we've walked
More than a mile

Within this broken heart of mine

Within this broken heart of mine
Lay memories of a love gone by
A love that was so strong
A love that kept me warm
The only love I've ever known
Within this broken heart of mine
A longing for the love that died
The love that I have cried for
The love that I would die for
Somehow my heart can't read between the lines
Now I sit at home alone
and pray that maybe he will phone
But what's the use, he's gone and I'm forlorn
He will never be mine, but this I know
His memory will stay there
Though the years fly by
Within this broken heart of mine

Breathless

You look at me
You smile that smile

You leave me breathless

You touch my hand
You speak my name

You leave me breathless

The thought of you
It does the same

You leave me breathless

Your fond hello
Sets me aglow

You leave me breathless

What would you do
If you knew

You leave me breathless

Georgia

Don't want to bake in the Arizona sun
Don't want to shake in a California quake
Don't want to go broke in Reno's casinos
Just want to live in Georgia
Don't want to lie beneath a Montana sky
Or walk the black hills of Dakota
Keep the tea in Boston harbor
Cause all the things I've come to love
Are all in the state of Georgia
Don't want to live on New England's rocky shores
Don't want to live behind luxury's doors
I just want to live in Georgia
The lonely wind whistling through the pines
Call me home wherever I may roam
To my hearth in Atlanta, Georgia

There is a Time

There is a time, there is a
season
for every purpose under
heaven
there is a reason

He is my source of light
He is my healer
He is my love of life
That's why I'm a believer

This is my time
I've found such pleasure
I feel a wondrous joy
within me
He is my treasure

He is my source of light
He is my healer
He is my love of life
That's why I'm a believer

This is the time to tell His
story
I raise my voice toward
heaven
to sing God's glory
He is my source of light
He is my healer
He is my love of life
That's why I'm a believer
That's why I'm a believer

Without You

If you can count the stars in the sky
Then you know how many ways I love you
If you can measure the circumference of the universe
Then you know how much I love you
If you can find the most beautiful of God's creations
Then you know how I feel when I am with you
And if you know when the last day of eternity is
Then you know, short one day
just how long I'll love you
And if you know what would happen to the earth
If it stopped turning on its axis
You know what my world was like without you

Summer

Summer is my favorite time of year
It's cotton candy
A merry Go round
and the county fair
Summer is baseball in the park
Long hot days
Long warm nights
And lovin' in the dark
Summer is swimming in the lake
Is the time of year
The old north wind
decides to take a break

Ever-changing life

Life is up, Life is down
Life is a merry go round
Round and round you go
Life is a series of changes
But one thing never changes
I want to happily everafter
with you
Life's a lesson
Life's a journey
Not made to take alone
And all thru Life
people come and go

Life is a series of changes
But one thing never changes
I want to happily ever after with
you
Life's a garden
Life's a banquet
Life's a dance
Be my partner
Life's a party
Life's a question
Always in search of answers
Happily everaftering with you

Heartsong

Heartsong the silent song
my aching heart sings to you
Heartsong says all the things
that I can't sing to you
across the miles, across the smiles
the haunting music of an aching heart

She was born way out in Oakland
I was large with child that day
It all seemed very much worth it
when in my arms she finally laid
My love's in Erin Taylor
Eyes of amber, green, and gold

My love's in Erin Taylor
And she's mine to have and hold
Hair of brown and lots of freckles
And her smile lights up my world
Full of energy and mischief
She's my precious little girl
My love's in Erin Taylor
Eyes of Amber, green, and gold
My love's in Erin Taylor
And she's mine to have and hold
Sure a little bit of heaven fell from out the sky one day
And she nestled right here in my arms.

Magic

Each time I close my eyes
I see your smiling face
It brings back that most magic moment
of my life
Hoping that you and I are not
Two ships passing in the night
Come spend time with me
we will walk the summer breeze
and if it doesn't work well
we'll be friends eternally
We live worlds apart
so let us close the miles
it would cheer my heart
to live with each of your smiles
We'll walk hand in hand
toe to toe we'll stand
shutting out both worlds
in our little land
Each time I close my eyes
I see your smiling face
It brings back that most magic moment
of my life

Love in your heart

The love in your heart
wasn't put there to stay
love isn't love
till you give it away
So give me your love
and I'll give it right back to you
Give my your lips
and I'll give you mine
my arms will be yours
till the end of time
give me your love and
I'll give it right back to you

Angelic Love

I wanna be wrapped in
the wings of angelic love
safe from the world outside
when the coldness of this world
creeps into my soul
and the claws of time
are tearing at my dreams
and all of my horizons
have all slipped away
I wanna be wrapped
in the wings of angelic love
safe from the world outside

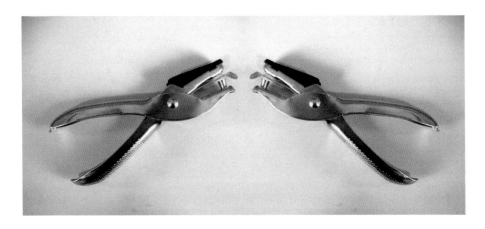

Show and Tell

Lets take an adventure
we'll explore each other well
we'll take down all the barriers
and we'll play show and tell
you show me your soul
and I'll show you mine
we can play this game together
till the end of time
Show and tell, we'll know each other well
show and tell, in the fields of time
we'll dwell
Lifetime after lifetime
no matter where we are
we'll find each other and
we'll play show and tell
From the mountains to the valleys
and from shore to shore
we'll trip the light fantastic
until time is no more
and beyond forever
the friendship never ends
we'll just keep on going
and do it all again

Lay my burden down

Looking back on fantasies and dreams
gone unfulfilled
Years of work that never brought reward
Looking longingly at heaven, and
a simpler time and place
Where I can finally lay my burden down
If heaven has a poppy field, that
I can wander through
You can bet I'll wander through
with you
Did my best in this old world
It wasn't good enough
I know there's a better world ahead
Heaven's highway – there's no better way
come and walk my way

Chasin' rainbows

Well, I'd love to be your darlin'
But you're the pot of gold at
the end of the rainbow
God in all His wisdom
created day and night
and a special time
for each to be
and here I am
in eternal twilight
wondering which one is for me
Rainbows are elusive
like butterflies and love
always round the corner
never close enough to touch

Bells

Bells, ringing bells, ringing loud, ringing long
Bells tinkling bells, is what I hear
when you are near
like a chapel chime, each time we meet
so pure and sweet, ringing in my ears.

Lovin' the blues away

It's a great day for lovin' the blues away
it's a great day for you and me
and the willow tree, down in the valley
where the river runs free
it's a great day for the lovin' the blues away
We can watch the clouds as they go by
we can sit and smile eye to eye
or pick daffodils of the country side
it's a great day for lovin' the blues away
We can watch the owl as he stares at us
we can watch the eagle as he soars above
we can watch each other as we fall in love

Gentle Rain (original)

You climbed inside me
you touched my very soul
and in that moment
That very moment
my world stopped cold
Your eyes, they showed me
a promise of yesteryear
a longing unfulfilled
through all the years
With a gentle rain from heaven
the seed of love does grow
one lovely little flower
waiting for the sun to sow
Again you went your separate way
never knowing what you'd done
leaving me with emptiness
the ended search has just begun

Salvation Shores

What would you do to land on salvation shores
would you reach out your hand
to a drowning man
Tossing and turning on a troubled sea
the way to salvation shores
will surely set you free
What would you do to land on salvation shores
would you turn the tide for your fellow man
Trying and crying thru life's stormy sea
the way to salvation shores
will surely set you free
What would you do to land on salvation shores
Caring and giving with an open heart
loving and living a life that's truly free
The way to salvation shores
is just across the sea

Yesteryear

As I leaf through an old and dusty scrap book in my mind
your eyes come back a haunting me of a lost forgotten time
A time when life was easy
a time when hearts were free
a time when all tomorrows
held dreams for you and me
I sit here in my memories
The years have come and gone
all of my tomorrows
are lost in golden songs
The radio keeps playing
the dreams that never were
the golden oldie station
again yesterday is clear
Oh whatever happened
to the promises we made
the plans of home and family

the hammock in the shade
now there'll be no one
to hold hands with on the porch
to sit and watch the sunset
and rekindle that old torch
the years have come and gone
the scrapbooks turned to dust
the promises unkept
and the world keeps turning round

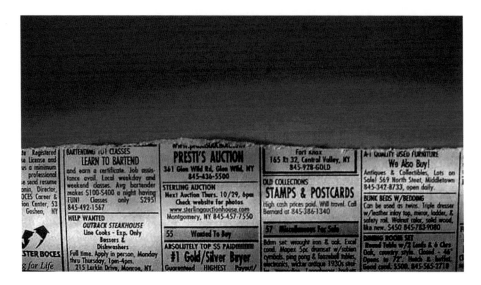

Ragged Edge

Walking on the ragged edge
It comes closer every day
nails are bitten to a nub
nerves shattered like broken clay
It seems my futures in the past
but your memory lingers on
walking on the ragged edge
and my time is nearly gone
If God's not listening to my prayers
then surely all is lost
I'm walking on the ragged edge
happiness is the cost
I don't want much in this ole world
just something to call mine
peace and quiet, a chance for love
four arms intertwined
Walking o the ragged edge
it comes closer every day
and all of this, for my sanity
I am forced to pay

Walking on the ragged edge
time and sanity
not knowing which one will give
which one will set me free
set me free of caring
or of life entirely

Surfaces

She was the prettiest girl I'd ever seen
Big blue eyes from the silver screen
Gave me a look that pierced my soul
I knew that this woman could make me whole

Lord knows I never look at blue eyes the same way again

So I gave her my best line
Walked right up and asked her sign
and this is what she said

I am weary of surfaces
only truth will do
So unless you get to know me
I won't go home with you

She said, now if you take your time
and get to know my mind

I said I'm just looking for a little fun
and you could use some too
I know that almost any guy
could take a spin with you

I am weary of surfaces
and since you have been true, I'll tell you
Everything you see is real, when you look at me
including the feelings you just hurt

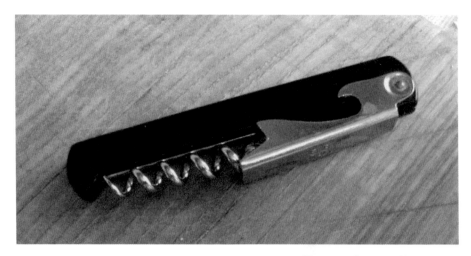

Lost in a dream

I think I lost you in a dream
I turned around and you were gone
I think I dreamed a bit too long
I thought I'd tell you in a song
If you'd come back I'd make you mine
You'd make my dull drab world to shine
And together we will be
Forever dreaming peacefully
There was time when I thought
dreaming was the only way
I could survive
This cold and callous world we live in
Is hard to take from day to day
Together this old world can't lick us
together through eternity
together we can face it bravely
together, just you and me
Until then I'll go on dreaming
Until then I'll dream alone
Come back and let me touch you
come back and make me feel
come back and be my man
come back and make me real

Coming Home

You reached out, you offered truth
you touched my heart, and I ran scared
You showed me you, that you were real
that no one else on earth compared
I ran, it was too real
I hid, so not to feel
but home is what you are
tho' I've never known a home
I am coming home, will you be there
will your arms open to embrace
will your lips part to meet mine
I'm coming home will you be there
my heart will break if you're not there
my arms will ache if you're not there
my soul will die if you're not there
Will you be there, I'm coming home
will you be there I'm coming home

Can't love without you

I can't love without you
You're all that I hold dear
I can't love without you
You're the music that I hear
You are the song in my heart
without you mornings wouldn't start
Life isn't life without meaning
and you are the meaning of my life
What's a day without the sun rising
What's a night without the stars shining
and what am I if you're not at my side

Knowing

You touched my heart
You searched my soul
not knowing what you'd find
But you fulfilled
through all the years
a special dream of mine
a dream for all times
I've tried so hard
Just to be heard
so much I had to say

Down through the years
I had to learn
that silence was the way
I've searched so long
For one like me
who listens with their eyes
who without words
would let me know
that he stands by my side

Gentle rain 3

Like a gentle rain from heaven
that is how your love makes me feel
like the clean fresh smell of springtime
refreshing, sweet, and real

You put your arms around me
all my troubles melt away
my heart soars like an eagle
my soul flies wild and free
Love used to be a shadow
sometimes seen, but never touched
and now loves sent me you dear
and I love you oh so much

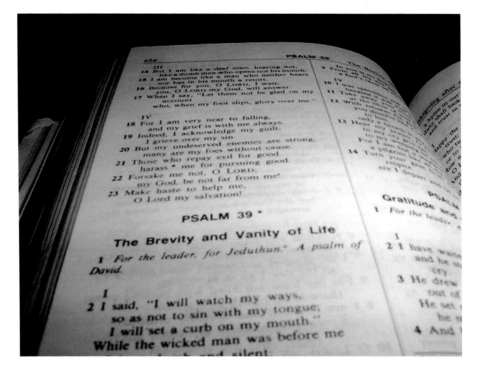

Yesterday's future

In the back of my mind is a fading memory
of a tomorrow that may never be
Deep in my heart is a distant longing
For a love I may never see
Down in my soul is the sound of God
telling me He is there and hang on
When will I do, instead of dream
When will I have, instead of want
When will I live and not exist
In my memory are a pair of green eyes
looking hauntingly back
and outstretched arms
once warm from holding me
Somewhere in the past
I left my future
Would that only
I could turn and go back

Time Passages

Winding down the passages
of flowers faded long ago
thinking of a man who
I wish I still could know
Remembering the feeling of
his fingers on my face
remembering when my heart
knew a gentler time and place

Walking through the pastureof
youth's promises and dreams
I see the name of each young man
who never gathered in his dreams
Promises and memories never kept
I'm looking hard at forty and
and back at dreams
I'll never know

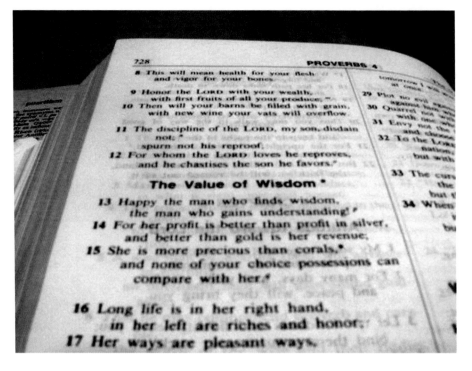

Wisdom of the ages

She rides the warm and gentle summer breeze
of the southland every day
She sprinkles seeds of hope that grow
into loves thornless rose in summertime
Looking at the flowers that were covered
with winter's barren snow
She delivers to a broken heart
the love that finally dries your tears
She is the wisdom of the ages
to love lost long ago
and plants the seeds of love
where they may freely grow
She is the spirit of freedom
that soars across the skies
planting the elusive rose of love

Fantasies

Fantasies, fantasies
come make mine all come true
I wouldn't have these fantasies
if it weren't for you

You stepped off the stage one night
and drew me in your arms
my room was just up one flight
I was captured by your charms
Never thought I'd see the day
I'd be so lost in love
flew back home but not to stay
tears filled the skies above

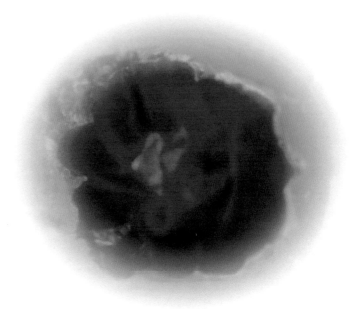

Roses, morning dew, and you

I am blazing a trail of thorns to you
In hopes that roses and morning dew
are all that I find when my journey is through
Roses, morning dew, and you

Roses, morning dew and you
sunshine in my coffee
and a kiss or two
roses, morning dew and you

I see so many things along the path
that beckon, I slow down and wait
but I know if I stray from the path
that when I get to you, you'll close the gate

Memory's Lane

Down my lane of memories
where you live in effigy
sweet as the day that we met
I vow never to forget

Through times passages
lessons learned through love
taught by carried messages
from one who lives above

when I see you in my dreams
you still whisper in my ear
it's not as bad as it seems
trust in the Lord my dear.

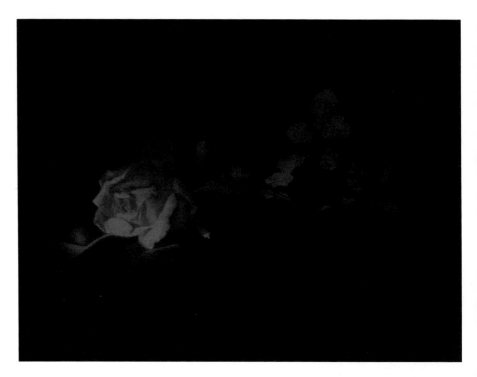

Crystal Roses

Crystal roses
how they tinkle
how they twinkle
how they shine

crystal roses
on my table
crystal tears
in my wine

Thank you …

for spending some of your precious time reading my poetry. As you go about this journey called life, remember to take good care of your heart and your feet, as they will always be your closest companions.

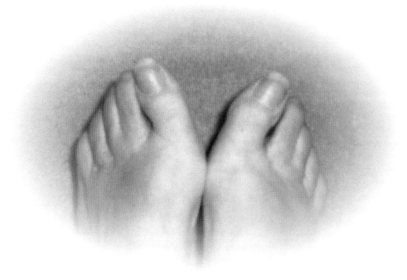

Time will tell a story
Etch it in your face
It will be one of glory
Or one of disgrace
It depends on how you
Choose to run the race

About the author

S. E. Blackstock was born in Boston, Massachusetts, and raised in the San Francisco Bay Area. Even after her relocation to the west coast, her strict Bostonian upbringing continued.

She started writing poems and songs in her late teens 'beginning with her very first heartbreak'. Her writing then extended to an exploration of God's wonders, and she has been writing for 40 plus years now.

Her poetry reveals a fascination for time and space and the wonders of the human soul. Her love of music is reflected in her poetry as many of the poems included here actually began as lyrics to songs.

She credits her many roles in life and her faith in God as sources of inspiration for her poetry, noting "I write from the perspective of a teenager, a woman, a lady, a mother, a lover, a friend, and a spirit-filled believer in Jesus Christ."

Proof

Made in the USA
Charleston, SC
23 February 2010